API-First Architecture for Everything-As-A-Service development with ASP.NET Web API

Table of Contents

Introduction

Welcome to the Journey

Welcome to 'API-First Architecture for Everything-As-A-Service development with ASP.NET Web API.' This book is designed to be a comprehensive guide for both beginners and experienced developers looking to adopt an API-First approach in their projects.

Why This Book?

APIs have become the backbone of modern software development, enabling seamless integration and communication between different services and applications. This book aims to provide you with the knowledge and tools needed to design, develop, and deploy APIs using ASP.NET Web API.

What Will You Learn?

1. **Understanding API-First Architecture**: Learn what it means to develop with an API-First mindset and why it's beneficial.

2. **ASP.NET Web API**: Get hands-on experience with one of the most powerful frameworks for building APIs.

3. **Security**: Understand various security mechanisms like OAuth2 and JWT.

4. **Advanced Topics**: Dive into more advanced topics like versioning, rate limiting, and microservices.

5. **Real-World Examples**: Gain insights from case studies that showcase the implementation of API-First Architecture in different industries.

Who Is This Book For?

This book is for anyone interested in API development, whether you're a student, a backend developer, or even a project manager. No prior experience with

ASP.NET Web API is required, although some familiarity with programming concepts will be helpful.

Let's Get Started!

So, are you ready to embark on this exciting journey? Let's get started!

Chapter 1: Introduction to API-First Architecture

The Pervasiveness of APIs in Modern Software Development

In the modern era of software development, the term "API" has become more than just a buzzword; it's a fundamental building block of any software ecosystem. APIs have evolved from being mere afterthoughts to becoming the central focus of software development. This chapter aims to provide an in-depth understanding of what API-First Architecture is and why it's crucial for modern software development. We will explore the evolution of APIs, the significance of adopting an API-First approach, and the myriad benefits it brings to the table.

What is an API?

An API, or Application Programming Interface, is a set of rules and protocols that allow different software entities to communicate with each other. It serves as a bridge between different software applications, enabling them to interact, exchange data, and perform various functions without requiring the end-user to be involved in the process. APIs have become the glue that holds the digital world together, enabling integrations between disparate systems and platforms.

The Historical Context: The Evolution of APIs

In the early days of software development, APIs were often an afterthought. Developers would first build the application and then think about how to expose certain functionalities via an API. However, this approach had its limitations:

1. **Scalability Issues**: As the application grew, it became increasingly difficult to manage and extend the API.

2. **Lack of Flexibility**: The API was tightly coupled with the application, making it hard to adapt to changing requirements.

3. **Poor Developer Experience**: Due to the lack of proper documentation and inconsistent design, developers found it challenging to integrate with the API.

The Paradigm Shift: The API-First Approach

The API-First Architecture turns the traditional approach on its head. Instead of building the API as an afterthought, it becomes the first-class citizen in the development process. The API is designed and built before the actual application, ensuring that it is robust, scalable, and flexible right from the get-go. This shift in focus brings about a cultural change within the development team, emphasizing the importance of the API in the overall architecture.

The Multifaceted Benefits of API-First Architecture

1. **Consistency**: By designing the API first, you ensure that it follows a consistent pattern, making it easier for developers to understand and work with.

2. **Scalability**: A well-designed API can easily accommodate future changes, making your application more scalable.

3. **Faster Time to Market**: With the API already in place, front-end and back-end developers can work in parallel, speeding up the development process.

4. **Improved Developer Experience**: A well-documented and consistent API improves the developer experience, encouraging more integrations and extensions.

Real-World Scenarios: The Ubiquity of APIs

1. **E-commerce Platforms**: Companies like Amazon and Shopify have robust APIs that allow third-party developers to create apps that enhance the platform's functionality.

2. **Social Media**: Platforms like Facebook and Hootsuite offer APIs for developers to create custom applications, analytics tools, or even bots.

3. **Financial Services**: Companies like Stripe help build economic infrastructure for the internet and provide APIs to all businesses handle payments and other financial operations.

The Necessity of API-First Architecture

API-First Architecture is not just a trend but a necessity in modern software development. It offers numerous benefits, including consistency, scalability, and improved developer experience. By adopting an API-First approach, organizations can build robust and flexible systems that are ready to meet the challenges of the ever-evolving tech landscape.

Setting the Stage for What's Next

This chapter serves as an introduction to the concept of API-First Architecture, setting the stage for the more detailed discussions in the subsequent chapters. We will delve into the technical aspects, best practices, and real-world applications of APIs, focusing on ASP.NET Web API as our primary framework.

Conclusion

This concludes the first chapter. The next chapter will focus on getting started with ASP.NET Web API, where we will guide you through setting up your first API project. We hope this chapter has provided you with a solid foundation and understanding of what API-First Architecture is and why it's so pivotal in today's software development landscape.

By the end of this book, you will have a comprehensive understanding of API-First Architecture and will be well-equipped to implement it in your own projects. So, let's embark on this exciting journey together!

Further Reading

1. "APIs: A Strategy Guide" by Daniel Jacobson, Greg Brail, and Dan Woods
2. "RESTful Web APIs" by Leonard Richardson, Mike Amundsen, and Sam Ruby
3. "Building Microservices" by Sam Newman

Chapter 2: Getting Started with ASP.NET Web API

In the previous chapter, we introduced the concept of API-First Architecture and its importance in modern software development. Now, it's time to roll up our sleeves and get our hands dirty with some actual coding. In this chapter, we will guide you through setting up your first ASP.NET Web API project. We'll cover everything from installing the necessary software to creating your first API endpoint.

Prerequisites

Before we dive in, make sure you have the following software installed on your machine:

1. **Visual Studio 2019 or later**

2. **.NET Core SDK 3.1 or later**

Setting Up Your Development Environment

First, open Visual Studio and create a new project. Select "ASP.NET Core Web Application" as the project template. Name your project and choose a suitable location to save it. On the next screen, select "API" and make sure that the "Enable Open API Support" checkbox is ticked. Click "Create" to generate your project.

Your First API Endpoint

Once the project is created, you'll see a folder structure on the left-hand side. Navigate to the Controllers folder and open the WeatherForecastController.cs file. This file contains a sample API controller with a single GET endpoint.

Code Example

Let's create a simple API to manage a list of string values. Replace the existing code in WeatherForecastController.cs with the following:

C#:

```csharp
using Microsoft.AspNetCore.Mvc;
using System.Collections.Generic;

namespace YourProjectName.Controllers
{
    [ApiController]
    [Route("[controller]")]
    public class ValuesController : ControllerBase
    {
        [HttpGet]
        public ActionResult<IEnumerable<string>> Get()
        {
            var values = new List<string> { "value1", "value2", "value3" };
            return Ok(values);
        }
    }
}
```

In this code snippet, we define a new API controller called **ValuesController**. We use the **[ApiController]** and **[Route]** attributes to specify that this class is an API controller and to define the route where it can be accessed. The **Get** method returns a list of string values.

Running Your API

To run your API, press F5 or click the "Start Debugging" button. Your API will start, and a new browser window will open displaying the Swagger UI, which is an interactive documentation for your API. You can test your API directly from this UI.

Expanding Your API

Now that we have a basic GET endpoint, let's add more functionalities:

1. **Adding a Value**:

   To add a new value to our list, we can use the HTTP POST method.

C#:

```csharp
[HttpPost]
public ActionResult<string> Post([FromBody] string value)
{
    var values = new List<string> { "value1", "value2", "value3" };
    values.Add(value);
    return Ok("Value added successfully");
}
```

In the above code, we added a method to insert a new value into our list. We use the **[HttpPost]** attribute to indicate that this method responds to HTTP POST requests. The method accepts a **value** parameter from the request body, which represents the value to be added. We then add this value to our static list. Finally, we return an **Ok** response indicating that the value was added successfully.

2. **Updating a Value**:

   To update an existing value in our list, we can use the HTTP PUT method.

C#:

```csharp
[HttpPut("{id}")]
public ActionResult<string> Put(int id, [FromBody] string newValue)
{
    var values = new List<string> { "value1", "value2", "value3" };
    if (id >= 0 && id < values.Count)
    {
        values[id] = newValue;
        return Ok("Value updated successfully");
    }
    return NotFound("Value not found");
}
```

In the above code, we added a method to update a specific value in our list based on its index. We use the **[HttpPut]** attribute with an **{id}** placeholder to indicate that this method responds to HTTP PUT requests and expects an **id** parameter in the URL. The method accepts two parameters: **id** (from the URL) and **newValue** (from the request body). We check if the **id** is valid (i.e., within the range of the list's indices). If it is, we update the corresponding value in the list with **newValue**.

If the update is successful, we return an **Ok** response with a success message. If the **id** is invalid, we return a **NotFound** response with an error message.

Error Handling and Validation

In a real-world application, you'll also need to handle errors and validate incoming data. ASP.NET Web API provides several ways to do this, such as model validation, custom filters, and exception handling mechanisms.

1. **Model Validation**:
   You can use data annotations to validate the model. For example, if you're expecting a string value that should not be empty, you can annotate it with **[Required]**.

2. **Custom Filters**:
   You can create custom filters to handle errors or perform specific actions before or after the execution of an action method.

3. **Exception Handling**:
   You can use try-catch blocks or create a global exception handler to manage exceptions effectively.

Testing the API

Once your API is up and running, the next step is to test it. You can use various tools like Postman, Swagger, or even write unit tests to ensure that your API is working as expected.

Conclusion

In this chapter, we've covered the basics of setting up an ASP.NET Web API project, creating your first API endpoint, and expanding it to handle various operations. We also touched upon important aspects like routing, model binding, and error handling. With this foundation, you're well-equipped to build robust and scalable APIs.

Further Reading

1. "Pro ASP.NET Web API: HTTP Web Services in ASP.NET" by Tugberk Ugurlu and Alexander Zeitler

2. "ASP.NET Web API 2: Building a REST Service from Start to Finish" by Jamie Kurtz and Brian Wortman

3. "C# 9 and .NET 5 – Modern Cross-Platform Development" by Mark J. Price

Chapter 3: RESTful Principles and ASP.NET Web API

In the previous chapters, we've laid the groundwork for understanding API-First Architecture and how to get started with ASP.NET Web API. Now, it's time to dive deeper into the principles that make an API truly RESTful. In this chapter, we will explore what RESTful architecture is, how it aligns with ASP.NET Web API, and how to implement it in your projects.

What is REST?

REST stands for Representational State Transfer. It is an architectural style for designing networked applications. RESTful APIs use HTTP as the communication protocol and are designed around standard HTTP methods like GET, POST, PUT, DELETE, etc. The idea is to use these methods in a way that aligns with the underlying principles of the protocol.

RESTful Principles

RESTful APIs are built around a set of guiding principles:

1. **Stateless**: Each request from a client to a server must contain all the information needed to understand and process the request. There should be no session state stored on the server between requests.

2. **Client-Server Architecture**: RESTful APIs adhere to the client-server model, which separates the user interface concerns from the data storage concerns.

3. **Uniform Interface**: RESTful APIs have a uniform and consistent interface, which helps in decoupling the client and server and making the architecture more modular and scalable.

4. **Stateless Communication**: All client-server operations should be stateless. The request from the client to the server should contain all the information that the server needs to fulfill that request.

5. **Resource-Based**: In REST architecture, a resource is an object or a service that can be accessed by the client. A resource has a URI (Uniform Resource Identifier), which is used to uniquely identify that resource.

6. **Stateless Communication**: All client-server operations should be stateless. The request from the client to the server should contain all the information that the server needs to fulfill that request.

Implementing RESTful Principles in ASP.NET Web API

ASP.NET Web API makes it easy to build RESTful APIs. Let's look at a more detailed code example to understand how to implement these principles.

Code Example

C#:

```csharp
using System.Collections.Generic;
using Microsoft.AspNetCore.Mvc;

namespace RESTfulExample.Controllers
{
    [ApiController]
    [Route("api/[controller]")]
    public class ProductsController : ControllerBase
    {
        // GET: api/products
        [HttpGet]
        public ActionResult<IEnumerable<string>> Get()
        {
            return new string[] { "Product1", "Product2" };
        }

        // GET: api/products/1
        [HttpGet("{id}")]
        public ActionResult<string> Get(int id)
        {
            return "Product" + id;
        }

        // POST: api/products
        [HttpPost]
        public void Post([FromBody] string value)
        {
            // Code to add the new product
        }

        // PUT: api/products/1
        [HttpPut("{id}")]
        public void Put(int id, [FromBody] string value)
        {
            // Code to update the product with id
        }

        // DELETE: api/products/1
        [HttpDelete("{id}")]
        public void Delete(int id)
        {
            // Code to delete the product with id
        }
    }
}
```

Code Explanation

The above code example demonstrates a simple RESTful API using ASP.NET Web API for a hypothetical **Products** resource. Let's break down the code to understand how it aligns with RESTful principles.

Namespace and Controller

The code starts by defining a namespace **RESTfulExample.Controllers** and a controller class **ProductsController** that inherits from **ControllerBase**. The **[ApiController]** and **[Route("api/[controller]")]** attributes specify that this class will serve as an API controller and define the route for the API.

HTTP Methods

The controller defines methods corresponding to HTTP verbs:

1. **GET**: The **Get()** method returns a list of products. It's mapped to the route **api/products**.

2. **GET with ID**: The **Get(int id)** method returns a single product based on its ID. It's mapped to the route **api/products/{id}**.

3. **POST**: The **Post([FromBody] string value)** method adds a new product. The new product data is passed in the request body.

4. **PUT**: The **Put(int id, [FromBody] string value)** method updates an existing product based on its ID. The updated data is passed in the request body.

5. **DELETE**: The **Delete(int id)** method deletes a product based on its ID.

Stateless Communication

The API is stateless, as each method contains all the information needed to process the request. There's no session state stored on the server between requests.

Resource-Based

The API is designed around the **Products** resource, which is accessed and manipulated using standard HTTP methods.

Conclusion

In this chapter, we've explored the principles of RESTful architecture and how they can be implemented using ASP.NET Web API. We've also looked at a detailed code example to understand how to design a RESTful API. Understanding these principles is crucial for building scalable, robust, and maintainable APIs.

Further Reading

1. "RESTful Web Services" by Leonard Richardson and Sam Ruby

2. "REST in Practice: Hypermedia and Systems Architecture" by Jim Webber, Savas Parastatidis, and Ian Robinson

3. "REST API Design Rulebook" by Mark Masse

Chapter 4: Authentication and Authorization in ASP.NET Web API

In the digital age, securing data and services is paramount. As APIs become the backbone of modern web and mobile applications, ensuring their security is non-negotiable. This chapter delves into the intricacies of authentication and authorization in ASP.NET Web API, providing a comprehensive understanding of how to safeguard your APIs.

Understanding Authentication and Authorization

At the heart of API security lie two concepts: authentication and authorization. While they are often used interchangeably, they serve distinct purposes:

- **Authentication**: Determines who you are. It verifies the identity of a user or system.

- **Authorization**: Determines what you can do. Once authenticated, it checks the permissions of a user or system.

The Need for Secure APIs

With the proliferation of cyber-attacks and data breaches, unsecured APIs are a significant vulnerability. They can expose sensitive data, allow unauthorized changes, and even lead to system takeovers. Hence, implementing robust authentication and authorization mechanisms is not just good practice—it's essential.

Diving Deep into JWT Authentication

JSON Web Tokens (JWT) have emerged as a popular standard for authentication in modern web applications. They offer a compact, self-contained mechanism for securely transmitting information between parties as a JSON object.

How JWT Works:

1. **Login**: Upon a successful login, the server generates a JWT that encodes user information and permissions, signs it, and sends it to the client.

2. **API Calls**: For subsequent API calls, the client attaches the JWT in the request header.

3. **Verification**: The server verifies the JWT's signature and, if valid, processes the request.

Implementing JWT in ASP.NET Web API:

ASP.NET Web API simplifies JWT authentication. Let's review an example of a basic implementation.

Code Example

C#:

```csharp
using Microsoft.AspNetCore.Authentication.JwtBearer;
using Microsoft.AspNetCore.Builder;
using Microsoft.Extensions.DependencyInjection;
using Microsoft.IdentityModel.Tokens;
using System.Text;

public void ConfigureServices(IServiceCollection services)
{
    var key = Encoding.ASCII.GetBytes("YourSecretKeyHere");
    services.AddAuthentication(x =>
    {
        x.DefaultAuthenticateScheme = JwtBearerDefaults.AuthenticationScheme;
        x.DefaultChallengeScheme = JwtBearerDefaults.AuthenticationScheme;
    })
    .AddJwtBearer(x =>
    {
        x.RequireHttpsMetadata = false;
        x.SaveToken = true;
        x.TokenValidationParameters = new TokenValidationParameters
        {
            ValidateIssuerSigningKey = true,
            IssuerSigningKey = new SymmetricSecurityKey(key),
            ValidateIssuer = false,
            ValidateAudience = false
        };
    });
}

public void Configure(IApplicationBuilder app)
{
    app.UseAuthentication();
}
```

Code Explanation

In this code:

- We first define a secret key for signing the JWT.

- We then set up JWT authentication, specifying the signing key and turning off issuer and audience validation for simplicity.

- Finally, we add the authentication middleware to our app's pipeline.

Role-Based Authorization

Beyond authentication, ASP.NET Web API also supports role-based authorization. This allows you to specify which roles can access specific API endpoints.

For instance, consider a blogging platform with roles like **Admin** and **Reader**. While both can read posts, perhaps only an **Admin** can create or delete them.

Code Example

Here's how you can implement role-based authorization:

C#:

```csharp
using Microsoft.AspNetCore.Authorization;
using Microsoft.AspNetCore.Mvc;

[Authorize(Roles = "Admin")]
public class BlogController : ControllerBase
{
    // This action can only be accessed by users with the Admin role
    public IActionResult CreatePost(PostModel post)
    {
        // Logic to create a new post
        return Ok();
    }

    // This action can be accessed by any authenticated user
    [Authorize]
    public IActionResult ReadPost(int postId)
    {
        // Logic to read a post
        return Ok();
    }
}
```

Code Explanation

In this example:

- The **BlogController** is decorated with **[Authorize(Roles = "Admin")]**, meaning all actions within this controller are accessible only to users with the **Admin** role.

- The **ReadPost** action is decorated with **[Authorize]**, making it accessible to any authenticated user, regardless of their role.

This approach allows you to implement fine-grained access control in your API, ensuring that users can only perform actions they are authorized to do.

Advanced Authorization Techniques

While role-based authorization is powerful, sometimes you need more granular control. ASP.NET Web API supports policy-based authorization, where you can define complex rules and conditions for accessing resources.

For example, you could define a policy that allows only users with an **Admin** role and those who have been a member for at least 30 days to delete posts.

Other Authentication and Authorization Mechanisms

JWT and role-based authorization are just the tip of the iceberg. ASP.NET Web API supports a plethora of other mechanisms:

- **OAuth2**: Widely used for third-party integrations, allowing applications to act on behalf of users.

- **OpenID Connect**: An extension of OAuth2, providing both authentication and authorization features.

- **API Keys**: Simple yet effective, especially for server-to-server authentication.

- **Basic Authentication**: Though less secure, it's still used in some legacy systems.

Best Practices

- **Always Use HTTPS**: This ensures that the data is encrypted during transit.

- **Store Secrets Securely**: Never hardcode secrets like your JWT signing key.

- **Implement Rate Limiting**: This can prevent abuse and secure your API further.

Conclusion

Securing your API is a critical aspect of API development. ASP.NET Web API offers a range of features to implement robust authentication and authorization mechanisms, helping you build secure, reliable, and scalable APIs. With a deep understanding of these concepts, you're well-equipped to take your API security to the next level.

In the next chapter, we'll explore API versioning, another crucial aspect of API development, to ensure backward compatibility and a smooth transition for your API consumers.

By the end of this chapter, you should have a comprehensive understanding of how to secure your APIs using ASP.NET Web API, setting the stage for more advanced topics in subsequent chapters.

Further Reading

1. "IdentityServer4 in Action" by Scott Brady and Dominick Baier

2. "OAuth 2.0 Simplified" by Aaron Parecki

3. "JSON Web Token (JWT) Handbook" by Auth0

Chapter 5: Versioning in Web API

API versioning is a critical aspect of API development and maintenance. As your API evolves, you'll likely introduce changes that could break existing clients. Versioning allows you to make these changes without affecting existing users, providing a smooth transition as your API grows and changes. This chapter will delve into the importance of API versioning, different strategies for implementing it, and how to manage versions effectively in ASP.NET Web API.

Why Versioning is Important

Imagine releasing an API that becomes widely adopted. You then decide to make a change, such as removing an endpoint or altering the data structure returned by an endpoint. Without versioning, these changes would break all the existing clients that rely on your API, leading to a poor developer experience and potential loss of trust.

Versioning allows you to introduce non-breaking changes, ensuring that existing clients can continue to function as expected while new clients can take advantage of the updated features.

Strategies for Versioning

There are several strategies for versioning an API, each with its pros and cons:

1. **URL Versioning**: The version information is included in the URL. For example, **/v1/users** and **/v2/users**.

2. **Header Versioning**: The version information is included in the HTTP header. This keeps the URL clean but requires the client to set the header correctly.

3. **Media Type Versioning**: The version information is included in the **Accept** header as a custom media type.

4. **Parameter Versioning**: The version information is included as a query parameter in the URL.

Versioning in ASP.NET Web API

ASP.NET Web API provides built-in support for API versioning. Let's explore how to implement URL versioning as it's one of the most straightforward and commonly used methods.

Code Example

C#:

```csharp
// Startup.cs

using Microsoft.AspNetCore.Mvc;
using Microsoft.Extensions.DependencyInjection;

public class Startup
{
    public void ConfigureServices(IServiceCollection services)
    {
        services.AddApiVersioning();
    }
}

// UsersController.cs

using Microsoft.AspNetCore.Mvc;

[ApiVersion("1.0")]
[Route("api/v{version:apiVersion}/users")]
public class UsersController : ControllerBase
{
    [HttpGet]
    public IActionResult GetUsersV1()
    {
        return Ok(new { Message = "Version 1" });
    }
}

// UsersControllerV2.cs

using Microsoft.AspNetCore.Mvc;

[ApiVersion("2.0")]
[Route("api/v{version:apiVersion}/users")]
public class UsersControllerV2 : ControllerBase
{
    [HttpGet]
    public IActionResult GetUsersV2()
    {
        return Ok(new { Message = "Version 2" });
    }
}
```

Code Explanation

In the code example above, we demonstrate how to implement URL versioning in an ASP.NET Web API project. Here's a breakdown of the code:

Startup.cs

In the **Startup** class, we add API versioning to the services collection using **services.AddApiVersioning();**. This enables the API versioning feature in the application.

UsersController.cs

1. We define an API version using the **[ApiVersion]** attribute and specify it as "1.0".

2. The **[Route]** attribute includes a version parameter **{version:apiVersion}** that dynamically picks up the API version.

3. The **GetUsersV1** method returns a message indicating its version 1 of the API.

UsersControllerV2.cs

1. Similar to **UsersController**, we define an API version as "2.0".

2. The **GetUsersV2** method returns a message indicating its version 2 of the API.

With this setup, you can access the different versions of the API by changing the version number in the URL. For example, to access version 1, you would use the URL **http://localhost:5000/api/v1/users**, and for version 2, **http://localhost:5000/api/v2/users**.

Pros and Cons of URL Versioning

Pros

1. **Simplicity**: It's straightforward and easy to understand.

2. **Visibility**: The version is clearly visible in the URL, making it easier to debug.

3. **Cacheability**: Since the version is part of the URL, responses can be easily cached.

Cons

1. **URL Pollution**: The URL contains version information, which some consider to be pollution.

2. **Client Dependency**: Clients need to update the URL when switching to a new version.

Conclusion

API versioning is essential for maintaining a robust and flexible API. ASP.NET Web API offers built-in support for various versioning strategies, making it easier to manage API versions effectively. URL versioning, as demonstrated, is one of the most commonly used methods due to its simplicity and visibility. However, the choice of versioning strategy may vary depending on your specific requirements and constraints.

Further Reading

1. "Web API Design: The Missing Link" by Brian Mulloy

2. "Versioning RESTful Services" by Peter Williams

3. "Continuous API Management" by Mehdi Medjaoui, Erik Wilde, Ronnie Mitra, and Mike Amundsen

Chapter 6: Data Serialization and Deserialization

Data serialization and deserialization are fundamental aspects of any API. Serialization is the process of converting complex data types like objects into a format that can be easily stored or transmitted and reconstructed later. Deserialization is the reverse process, where the serialized data is converted back into its original form. In the context of APIs, serialization and deserialization are crucial for data exchange between the client and the server.

In this chapter, we will explore how ASP.NET Web API handles data serialization and deserialization, focusing on popular data formats like JSON and XML. We will also look at customization options and best practices.

Why Serialization and Deserialization are Important

1. **Data Exchange**: APIs often need to send or receive data in a format that both the client and server understand. Serialization and deserialization facilitate this data exchange.

2. **Data Integrity**: Proper serialization ensures that the data maintains its integrity during transmission.

3. **Flexibility**: Different clients may require data in different formats. A well-designed API should be able to serialize data into multiple formats.

Common Data Formats

JSON (JavaScript Object Notation)

JSON is a lightweight data-interchange format that is easy to read and write. It is based on a subset of JavaScript and is language-independent.

XML (eXtensible Markup Language)

XML is a markup language that defines rules for encoding documents in a format that is both human-readable and machine-readable. It is often used for configuration files and data interchange.

Serialization and Deserialization in ASP.NET Web API

ASP.NET Web API uses the Newtonsoft.Json library for JSON serialization and the DataContractSerializer for XML serialization. Let's look at a code example to understand how this works.

Code Example

C#:

```csharp
using Microsoft.AspNetCore.Mvc;
using Newtonsoft.Json;

[Route("api/[controller]")]
public class DataController : ControllerBase
{
    [HttpGet("json")]
    public IActionResult GetJsonData()
    {
        var data = new { Name = "John", Age = 30 };
        var jsonData = JsonConvert.SerializeObject(data);
        return Ok(jsonData);
    }

    [HttpGet("xml")]
    public IActionResult GetXmlData()
    {
        var data = new { Name = "John", Age = 30 };
        var xmlData = SerializeToXml(data);
        return Ok(xmlData);
    }

    private string SerializeToXml(object obj)
    {
        // XML serialization logic here
        return "<xml></xml>"; // Placeholder
    }
}
```

Code Explanation

In the code example, we have a **DataController** with two endpoints: one for JSON data (**/api/data/json**) and one for XML data (**/api/data/xml**).

1. **JSON Endpoint**: We use the **JsonConvert.SerializeObject** method from the Newtonsoft.Json library to serialize the data object into a JSON string.

2. **XML Endpoint**: We use a custom method **SerializeToXml** to handle XML serialization. This is a placeholder; in a real application, you would use a library like **DataContractSerializer**.

Customization and Best Practices

1. **Custom Serialization**: You can create custom JSON converters or XML serializers to handle complex data types.

2. **Error Handling**: Implement proper error handling to deal with serialization or deserialization failures.

3. **Performance**: Be mindful of the performance implications of serialization, especially when dealing with large data sets.

Conclusion

Understanding data serialization and deserialization is crucial for API development. ASP.NET Web API provides robust support for handling various data formats, making it easier to build flexible and efficient APIs. By following best practices and leveraging customization options, you can create APIs that meet diverse client needs while maintaining data integrity and performance.

Further Reading

1. "Data-Intensive Text Processing with MapReduce" by Jimmy Lin and Chris Dyer

2. "Streaming, Sharing, Stealing: Big Data and the Future of Entertainment" by Michael D. Smith and Rahul Telang

3. "JSON at Work: Practical Data Integration for the Web" by Tom Marrs

Chapter 7: Rate Limiting and Throttling

Rate limiting and throttling are essential mechanisms for controlling the usage of an API. They ensure that the API remains available, responsive, and secure by limiting the number of requests a client can make within a specified time frame. This chapter will delve into the importance of rate limiting and throttling, how to implement them in ASP.NET Web API, and best practices for effective usage.

The Need for Rate Limiting and Throttling

In an ideal world, all users would use your API responsibly. However, the reality is far from it. Without proper controls, your API could be susceptible to abuse, leading to degraded performance, increased costs, and even security risks. Here are some reasons why rate limiting and throttling are indispensable:

1. **Resource Optimization**: APIs have limited resources, including bandwidth, memory, and processing power. Rate limiting ensures that these resources are used optimally.

2. **Fair Usage**: Without rate limiting, a single user or service could monopolize the API, leading to poor performance for other users.

3. **Security**: Throttling can act as a first line of defense against various types of attacks, such as DDoS attacks.

4. **Cost Control**: APIs often have associated costs, like third-party services or cloud computing charges. Limiting the rate of API calls can help in controlling these costs.

5. **Quality of Service**: By controlling the rate of requests, you can ensure a consistent and high-quality experience for all users.

Types of Rates Limiting

Rate limiting can be implemented in various ways, each with its own set of advantages and disadvantages. Here are some common types:

1. **Request Rate Limiting**: This is the most straightforward type, where the number of API calls is limited per time unit (e.g., 100 requests per minute).

2. **Concurrent Rate Limiting**: This type limits the number of simultaneous connections to the API.

3. **Bandwidth Limiting**: Here, the amount of data transferred is limited rather than the number of requests.

4. **Token Bucket Algorithm**: This is a more flexible approach where tokens are added to a 'bucket' at a fixed rate. Each API call consumes a token, and if the bucket is empty, the request is throttled.

5. **Leaky Bucket Algorithm**: Similar to the Token Bucket but designed to smooth out bursty traffic patterns.

6. **Quota-Based Limiting**: In this type, each user is given a fixed quota of API calls that can be used within a specific time frame.

Code Example

C#:

```csharp
using System;
using System.Collections.Generic;
using System.Threading;

// Token Bucket Algorithm Implementation
public class TokenBucket
{
    private readonly int _maxTokens;
    private readonly int _refillRate;
    private int _currentTokens;
    private DateTime _lastRefillTime;

    public TokenBucket(int maxTokens, int refillRate)
    {
        _maxTokens = maxTokens;
        _refillRate = refillRate;
        _currentTokens = maxTokens;
        _lastRefillTime = DateTime.UtcNow;
    }

    public bool AllowRequest()
    {
        Refill();
        if (_currentTokens > 0)
        {
            _currentTokens--;
            return true;
        }
        return false;
    }

    private void Refill()
    {
        var now = DateTime.UtcNow;
        var timePassed = (now - _lastRefillTime).TotalSeconds;
        var tokensToAdd = (int)(timePassed * _refillRate);
        _currentTokens = Math.Min(_currentTokens + tokensToAdd, _maxTokens);
        _lastRefillTime = now;
    }
}

// Example usage
public class Program
{
    public static void Main()
    {
        var bucket = new TokenBucket(10, 1);
        while (true)
        {
            if (bucket.AllowRequest())
            {
                Console.WriteLine("Request allowed at " + DateTime.UtcNow);
            }
            else
            {
                Console.WriteLine("Request denied at " + DateTime.UtcNow);
            }
            Thread.Sleep(500);
        }
    }
```

Code Explanation

The above code example demonstrates a simple implementation of the Token Bucket algorithm for rate limiting. Let's break down the code to understand how it works:

1. **TokenBucket Class**: This class is responsible for managing the tokens. It has private fields for the maximum number of tokens (**_maxTokens**), the refill rate (**_refillRate**), the current number of tokens (**_currentTokens**), and the last refill time (**_lastRefillTime**).

2. **Constructor**: The constructor initializes the TokenBucket with a maximum number of tokens and a refill rate. It also sets the **_currentTokens** to the maximum and initializes **_lastRefillTime** to the current time.

3. **AllowRequest Method**: This method is called to check if a request is allowed. It first calls the **Refill** method to add new tokens if needed. Then, it decrements **_currentTokens** by 1 if there are tokens available and returns **true**. Otherwise, it returns **false**.

4. **Refill Method**: This method calculates the number of tokens to add based on the time passed since the last refill. It then adds the tokens to **_currentTokens**, ensuring it doesn't exceed **_maxTokens**.

5. **Program Class**: This is an example usage of the TokenBucket class. It creates a new TokenBucket with a maximum of 10 tokens and a refill rate of 1 token per second. It then enters an infinite loop, checking if a request is allowed every 500 milliseconds.

Pros and Cons

Pros

1. **Flexibility**: The Token Bucket algorithm is flexible and can handle bursty traffic.

2. **Fairness**: It ensures that all users get a fair share of the available rate limit.

3. **Simplicity**: The algorithm is simple to understand and implement.

Cons

1. **Resource Consumption**: The algorithm requires storing state for each user, which can be resource-intensive for large-scale APIs.

2. **Time-Dependent**: The algorithm relies on system time, making it susceptible to clock drifts.

3. **Initial Burst**: If the bucket is full, it allows a burst of requests, which might not be desirable in all scenarios.

Implementing Rate Limiting in ASP.NET Web API

ASP.NET Web API provides built-in support for implementing rate limiting, but you can also use third-party libraries for more advanced features. Here's a step-by-step guide on how to implement basic rate limiting using ASP.NET Web API:

1. **Install Required Packages**: First, you'll need to install the necessary NuGet packages. For this example, we'll use **AspNetWebApi-RateLimit**.

bash:

```bash
Install-Package AspNetWebApi-RateLimit
```

2. **Configure Rate Limiting**: Open the **WebApiConfig.cs** file and add the following code to configure rate limiting.

```csharp
public static class WebApiConfig
{
    public static void Register(HttpConfiguration config)
    {
        // Other configurations

        // Configure rate limiting
        config.MessageHandlers.Add(new RateLimitHandler()
        {
            Policy = new RateLimitPolicy(perMinute: 5, perHour: 100)
        });
    }
}
```

3. **Test the API**: Once the rate limiting is configured, you can test it by sending multiple requests to your API. If you exceed the limit, you'll receive a **429 Too Many Requests** response.

Pros and Cons

Pros

1. **Ease of Use**: ASP.NET Web API makes it easy to implement rate limiting with just a few lines of code.

2. **Extensibility**: You can easily extend the built-in rate limiting features or use third-party libraries for more advanced scenarios.

3. **Integration**: Being a part of the ASP.NET ecosystem, it integrates seamlessly with other ASP.NET features like logging, caching, etc.

Cons

1. **Limited Features**: The built-in rate limiting features may not cover all scenarios, requiring you to use third-party libraries.

2. **Performance Overhead**: Adding rate limiting adds an extra layer of processing to each API request, which could impact performance if not implemented efficiently.

Best Practices for Rate Limiting

Implementing rate limiting is not just about adding a few lines of code; it's also about understanding the user behavior and the API's capabilities. Here are some best practices to consider:

1. **Transparent Policies**: Always make your rate limiting policies clear and easily accessible to the API consumers. This helps them understand the limitations and plan their usage accordingly.

2. **Graceful Degradation**: Instead of abruptly denying requests, consider implementing a system that gradually reduces the service level for over-limit users.

3. **Dynamic Limits**: Use dynamic rate limits that can be adjusted in real-time based on the system load or other metrics.

4. **Whitelisting and Blacklisting**: Have provisions for whitelisting trusted clients and blacklisting malicious ones.

5. **Logging and Monitoring**: Keep detailed logs of rate-limited requests and set up alerts for unusual activity.

6. **User Feedback**: Provide meaningful error messages and HTTP status codes to indicate rate-limited requests. The HTTP **429 Too Many Requests** status code is commonly used for this purpose.

7. **Rate Limit Headers**: Include HTTP headers to indicate the remaining number of requests and the time until the rate limit resets. This is useful for API consumers to manage their requests.

8. **Testing**: Thoroughly test the rate limiting implementation under various scenarios to ensure it works as expected and doesn't introduce new issues.

9. **Documentation**: Update the API documentation to include details about rate limiting, including the types of rate limiting used, the limits, and how to handle rate-limited responses.

10. **Review and Update**: Periodically review the rate limiting settings and make adjustments as needed, especially when launching new features or observing changes in user behavior.

Conclusion

Rate limiting and throttling are not just technical requirements but strategic tools that can help you manage your API effectively. They ensure that your API can serve as many users as possible in a fair and efficient manner, while also providing a layer of security against potential abuse. The Token Bucket algorithm, as demonstrated, is one of the many algorithms you can use to implement rate limiting. It's crucial to choose an algorithm and strategy that aligns with your API's usage patterns and requirements.

In ASP.NET Web API, implementing rate limiting is straightforward, but it's essential to consider the broader picture, including user experience and system performance. By following best practices like transparent policies, graceful degradation, and dynamic limits, you can create a robust and user-friendly API.

This chapter has provided you with the foundational knowledge and practical skills needed to implement rate limiting and throttling in your ASP.NET Web API projects. As you move forward, keep in mind that rate limiting is not a set-it-and-forget-it feature. It requires ongoing monitoring, tweaking, and possibly even some user education to get it just right.

Further Reading

1. "Rate Limiting in API Design: How to Build a Sustainable API" by Kristopher Sandoval

2. "API Rate Limiting with Redis" by Jos Dirksen

3. "Throttling APIs" by Microsoft Docs

Chapter 8: Testing Your API

Testing is an integral part of the software development lifecycle, and APIs are no exception to this rule. Ensuring that your API works as expected under various conditions is crucial for providing a reliable service. This chapter will introduce you to the tools and frameworks for testing your API built with ASP.NET Web API. We will cover unit testing, integration testing, and using Postman for manual testing.

Importance of Testing in API Development

Before diving into the technical aspects, let's understand why testing is essential in API development:

1. **Quality Assurance**: Testing ensures that your API is robust and works as expected.

2. **Early Bug Detection**: The sooner you find issues, the easier and cheaper they are to fix.

3. **Documentation**: Tests can serve as a form of documentation, showing how the API is supposed to work.

4. **Ease of Maintenance**: Well-tested APIs are easier to refactor, extend, and maintain.

Types of Testing

There are several types of tests you can perform on your API:

1. **Unit Tests**: These tests focus on individual components of your API, like controllers and models.

2. **Integration Tests**: These tests check the interaction between different parts of your system, including external services.

3. **End-to-End Tests**: These tests simulate real-world scenarios to validate the entire process flow.

4. **Load Tests**: These tests check how your API performs under heavy load.

Unit Testing in ASP.NET Web API

ASP.NET Web API integrates seamlessly with testing frameworks like MSTest, NUnit, and xUnit. For this example, we'll use MSTest.

Setting Up MSTest

First, you need to add a new MSTest Test Project to your solution. Then, add a reference to your Web API project.

Writing Your First Unit Test

Let's say you have a simple **Get** method in your **ProductsController** that returns a list of products. Here's how you can test it:

Code Example

C#:

```csharp
[TestClass]
public class ProductsControllerTest
{
    [TestMethod]
    public void TestGetProducts()
    {
        // Arrange
        var controller = new ProductsController();

        // Act
        var result = controller.Get();

        // Assert
        Assert.IsNotNull(result);
        Assert.AreEqual(5, result.Count());
    }
}
```

In this test, we first create an instance of **ProductsController**. Then, we call the **Get** method and check if it returns the expected results.

Integration Testing

Integration tests are more complex as they involve multiple components. You can use libraries like **WebApplicationFactory** to create a test server for running integration tests.

Code Example

Here's an example of an integration test that checks if the **Get** method returns a **200 OK** status.

C#:

```csharp
public class IntegrationTests : IClassFixture<WebApplicationFactory<Startup>>
{
    private readonly WebApplicationFactory<Startup> _factory;

    public IntegrationTests(WebApplicationFactory<Startup> factory)
    {
        _factory = factory;
    }

    [Fact]
    public async Task GetProducts_ReturnsOkStatus()
    {
        // Arrange
        var client = _factory.CreateClient();

        // Act
        var response = await client.GetAsync("/api/products");

        // Assert
        Assert.Equal(HttpStatusCode.OK, response.StatusCode);
    }
}
```

Manual Testing with Postman

Postman is a popular tool for API testing that provides a user-friendly interface for sending requests to your API. You can create collections, write tests, and even automate your testing process.

How to Use Postman

1. **Install Postman**: Download and install Postman from their official website.

2. **Create a New Collection**: This will hold all your API requests.

3. **Add Requests**: Add different API requests like GET, POST, PUT, DELETE to your collection.

4. **Run Tests**: You can write tests in JavaScript to validate the API responses.

Conclusion

Testing is not just a phase in API development; it's a continuous activity that ensures the reliability and robustness of your API. From unit tests that validate individual components to integration tests that ensure seamless interaction between components, each testing layer adds a level of confidence in your API. Tools like Postman further simplify the process by providing a platform for manual and automated testing.

By now, you should have a good understanding of how to test your API in ASP.NET Web API. The examples provided should serve as a starting point for writing your tests, and the tools discussed will help you in automating and managing your tests.

Further Reading

1. "The Art of Unit Testing" by Roy Osherove

2. "Testing ASP.NET Web API" by Badrinarayanan Lakshmiraghavan

3. "Postman for API Testing" by Valentin Despa

Chapter 9: Logging and Monitoring

Logging and monitoring are essential aspects of any production-grade API. They not only help in debugging and troubleshooting but also provide valuable insights into how your API is being used. This chapter will guide you through implementing logging and monitoring in your ASP.NET Web API project, covering various tools and best practices.

Why Logging and Monitoring?

Before diving into the technicalities, let's understand why logging and monitoring are crucial:

1. **Debugging**: Logs provide detailed information that can help you debug issues in your API.

2. **Performance Monitoring**: Monitoring tools can help you understand the performance characteristics of your API, helping you make informed decisions.

3. **Security**: Logs can be analyzed to detect unauthorized access or other security threats.

4. **Compliance**: For some industries, logging and monitoring are not optional but a regulatory requirement.

Types of Logs

There are several types of logs that you might want to consider:

1. **Access Logs**: These logs contain information about who accessed your API and what they accessed.

2. **Error Logs**: These logs contain information about errors that occurred while processing a request.

3. **Audit Logs**: These logs contain a history of changes made to the system.

4. **Diagnostic Logs**: These logs contain detailed information useful for debugging.

Logging in ASP.NET Web API

ASP.NET Web API provides built-in support for logging through its **ILogger** interface. You can also use third-party libraries like NLog, Serilog, or log4net.

Code Example

Using ILogger

Let's start by adding logging to a simple **ProductsController**:

C#:

```csharp
public class ProductsController : ApiController
{
    private readonly ILogger<ProductsController> _logger;

    public ProductsController(ILogger<ProductsController> logger)
    {
        _logger = logger;
    }

    public IEnumerable<Product> Get()
    {
        _logger.LogInformation("Getting all products");
        // Fetch products from database
        return new List<Product>();
    }

    public Product Get(int id)
    {
        _logger.LogInformation($"Getting product with ID {id}");
        // Fetch product by ID from database
        return new Product();
    }
}
```

Code Explanation

In this example, we inject an **ILogger<ProductsController>** into our controller and use it to log information. The **ILogger** interface provides methods like **LogInformation**, **LogWarning**, **LogError**, and **LogCritical** to log messages at different levels.

Monitoring with Application Insights

Application Insights is a cloud-based monitoring tool from Microsoft that integrates seamlessly with ASP.NET Web API. It provides features like request tracking, exception tracking, and custom events.

Setting Up Application Insights

1. **Install NuGet Package**: Install the **Microsoft.ApplicationInsights.AspNetCore** NuGet package.

2. **Initialize in Startup**: Add the following code to your **Startup.cs**:

C#:

```csharp
public void ConfigureServices(IServiceCollection services)
{

services.AddApplicationInsightsTelemetry(Configuration["ApplicationInsights:InstrumentationKey"]);
}
```

3. **Instrumentation Key**: Replace **InstrumentationKey** with the key from your Application Insights resource in Azure.

Using Application Insights

Once set up, Application Insights automatically starts collecting data. You can also track custom events:

C#:

```csharp
public class ProductsController : ApiController
{
    private readonly TelemetryClient _telemetryClient;

    public ProductsController(TelemetryClient telemetryClient)
    {
        _telemetryClient = telemetryClient;
    }

    public Product Get(int id)
    {
        _telemetryClient.TrackEvent("ProductFetched", new Dictionary<string, string>
        {
            { "ProductId", id.ToString() }
        });
        // Fetch product by ID from database
        return new Product();
    }
}
```

Code Explanation

In this example, we use **TelemetryClient** to send a custom event named **ProductFetched** to Application Insights.

Conclusion

Logging and monitoring are not just about collecting data but making sense of that data to improve your API. ASP.NET Web API provides robust logging capabilities through its **ILogger** interface, and tools like Application Insights offer comprehensive monitoring solutions. By implementing logging and monitoring, you not only improve the reliability and security of your API but also gain valuable insights into its usage and performance.

Further Reading

1. "Monitoring and Observability" by Cindy Sridharan

2. "The Art of Logging" by K. Scott Allen

3. "Application Insights for ASP.NET Core applications" by Microsoft Docs

Chapter 10: Microservices and ASP.NET Web API

The microservices architecture has gained significant traction in recent years, offering a way to build applications as a collection of loosely coupled, independently deployable services. This chapter will introduce you to the concept of microservices and guide you through building a simple microservice using ASP.NET Web API.

Why Microservices?

Before diving into the technical details, let's understand why microservices are essential:

1. **Scalability**: Microservices can be independently scaled, allowing for more efficient use of resources.

2. **Flexibility**: Different services can be written in different programming languages and can use different data storage technologies.

3. **Ease of Deployment**: Individual services can be deployed independently, making it easier to manage updates and rollbacks.

4. **Fault Isolation**: A failure in one service doesn't necessarily bring down the entire application.

Characteristics of a Microservice

1. **Single Responsibility**: Each microservice should have a single responsibility or function.

2. **Independently Deployable**: A microservice should be deployable independently of other services.

3. **Decentralized Data Management**: Each microservice should own its data and be the sole authority for its dataset.

4. **Statelessness**: Microservices should be stateless, meaning each request should contain all the information needed to process it.

Building a Simple Product Microservice

Let's build a simple Product microservice using ASP.NET Web API. This service will have endpoints to create, read, update, and delete (CRUD) products.

Code Example

Setting Up the Project

Create a new ASP.NET Web API project and name it **ProductMicroservice**.

Defining the Model

Create a **Product** model with properties like **Id**, **Name**, and **Price**.

C#:

```csharp
public class Product
{
    public int Id { get; set; }
    public string Name { get; set; }
    public decimal Price { get; set; }
}
```

Creating the Controller

Create a **ProductsController** with CRUD operations.

C#:

```csharp
[ApiController]
[Route("api/[controller]")]
public class ProductsController : ControllerBase
{
    private static List<Product> _products = new List<Product>
    {
        new Product { Id = 1, Name = "Laptop", Price = 1000 },
        new Product { Id = 2, Name = "Phone", Price = 500 }
    };

    [HttpGet]
    public ActionResult<IEnumerable<Product>> GetProducts()
    {
        return _products;
    }

    [HttpGet("{id}")]
    public ActionResult<Product> GetProduct(int id)
    {
        var product = _products.FirstOrDefault(p => p.Id == id);
        if (product == null)
        {
            return NotFound();
        }
        return product;
    }
```

```csharp
    [HttpPost]
    public ActionResult<Product> CreateProduct(Product product)
    {
        _products.Add(product);
        return CreatedAtAction(nameof(GetProduct), new { id = product.Id }, product);
    }

    // Implement Update and Delete methods
}
```

In this example, we define a static list of products to simulate a database. We then implement **HttpGet** methods to fetch all products and a single product by its ID. The **HttpPost** method is used to create a new product.

Deploying the Microservice

Once your microservice is ready, you can deploy it using various methods like Docker containers, Kubernetes, or Azure Kubernetes Service (AKS).

Dockerizing the Microservice

1. **Create a Dockerfile**: Create a **Dockerfile** in the root directory of your project.

2. **Build the Image**: Run **docker build -t product-microservice .** to build the Docker image.

3. **Run the Container**: Run **docker run -p 8080:80 product-microservice** to start the container.

Deploying to Kubernetes

If you have a Kubernetes cluster, you can deploy your Dockerized microservice using a Kubernetes Deployment.

yaml:

```yaml
apiVersion: apps/v1
kind: Deployment
metadata:
  name: product-microservice
spec:
  replicas: 3
  selector:
    matchLabels:
      app: product-microservice
  template:
    metadata:
      labels:
        app: product-microservice
    spec:
      containers:
        - name: product-microservice
          image: product-microservice:latest
```

Conclusion

Microservices offer a way to build scalable, flexible, and robust applications. ASP.NET Web API provides the necessary features to build RESTful microservices easily. By following best practices and using modern deployment methods, you can build a production-ready microservice.

Further Reading

1. "Building Microservices" by Sam Newman

2. "Microservices in .NET Core" by Christian Horsdal

3. "Kubernetes: Up and Running" by Kelsey Hightower

Chapter 11: Everything-As-A-Service (XaaS) Paradigm

The Everything-As-A-Service (XaaS) paradigm is an expansive approach to cloud computing and service-oriented architecture. It encompasses a wide range of services and technologies that can be delivered over the internet. This chapter will delve into the XaaS model, its various forms, and how it aligns with API-First Architecture, particularly in the context of ASP.NET Web API.

What is XaaS?

XaaS, or Everything-As-A-Service, is a collective term that includes any service, function, or feature that can be provided over the internet. This can range from traditional Software-as-a-Service (SaaS) offerings to more specialized services like Function-as-a-Service (FaaS), Backend-as-a-Service (BaaS), and many more.

Why XaaS Matters?

Here are some reasons why XaaS is gaining traction:

1. **Scalability**: XaaS allows businesses to scale services according to demand.

2. **Cost-Efficiency**: It eliminates the need for heavy upfront investment in infrastructure.

3. **Flexibility**: Businesses can choose from a wide array of services to meet specific needs.

4. **Speed**: Rapid provisioning of services speeds up the development and deployment cycles.

Types of XaaS

While SaaS, PaaS (Platform-as-a-Service), and IaaS (Infrastructure-as-a-Service) are the most commonly known types, the XaaS model includes a variety of other services:

1. **FaaS (Function-as-a-Service)**: Allows running individual functions in the cloud.

2. **BaaS (Backend-as-a-Service)**: Provides a ready-to-use backend for mobile and web applications.

3. **DaaS (Database-as-a-Service)**: Database solutions provided over the cloud.

4. **MLaaS (Machine Learning-as-a-Service)**: Offers machine learning tools as cloud services.

XaaS and API-First Architecture

In a XaaS model, APIs are the linchpin. They serve as the interface through which services are consumed. Therefore, adopting an API-First Architecture is not just beneficial but essential in a XaaS environment.

Creating a DaaS with ASP.NET Web API

Let's create a simple Database-as-a-Service (DaaS) using ASP.NET Web API. This service will expose an API to perform CRUD operations on a database.

Code Example

Setting Up the Project

Create a new ASP.NET Web API project and name it **SimpleDaaS**.

Defining the Model

Create a **Record** model with properties like **Id**, **Name**, and **Data**.

C#:

```csharp
public class Record
{
    public int Id { get; set; }
    public string Name { get; set; }
    public string Data { get; set; }
}
```

Creating the Controller

Create a **RecordsController** with CRUD operations.

C#:

```csharp
[ApiController]
[Route("api/[controller]")]
public class RecordsController : ControllerBase
{
    private readonly DatabaseContext _context;

    public RecordsController(DatabaseContext context)
    {
        _context = context;
    }

    [HttpGet]
    public ActionResult<IEnumerable<Record>> GetRecords()
    {
        return _context.Records.ToList();
    }

    [HttpGet("{id}")]
    public ActionResult<Record> GetRecord(int id)
    {
        var record = _context.Records.Find(id);
        if (record == null)
        {
            return NotFound();
        }
        return record;
```

```csharp
    }

    [HttpPost]
    public ActionResult<Record> CreateRecord(Record record)
    {
        _context.Records.Add(record);
        _context.SaveChanges();
        return CreatedAtAction(nameof(GetRecord), new { id = record.Id }, record);
    }

    // Implement Update and Delete methods
}
```

In this example, we use Entity Framework Core to interact with the database. The
RecordsController exposes endpoints to fetch all records, fetch a single record by
its ID, and create a new record.

Deploying Your DaaS

Once your DaaS is ready, you can deploy it using various methods like Docker
containers, Kubernetes, or Azure Kubernetes Service (AKS), similar to the
microservices example in the previous chapter.

Conclusion

The XaaS model is reshaping how businesses think about IT services and
infrastructure. It offers unparalleled flexibility, scalability, and cost-efficiency.
APIs, being the building blocks of XaaS, need to be designed with an API-First
Architecture to ensure they are robust, scalable, and easy to consume. ASP.NET
Web API provides all the necessary features to build such APIs, making it an
excellent choice for implementing various XaaS services.

Further Reading

1. "Cloud Computing Explained: SaaS, PaaS, and IaaS" by John Rhoton

2. "APIs: A Strategy Guide" by Daniel Jacobson, Greg Brail, and Dan Woods

3. "Microservices: Flexible Software Architecture" by Eberhard Wolff

Chapter 12: Deploying Your API

Deploying an API is a critical step in the development lifecycle. It's the point where your API becomes accessible to other developers, applications, or services. This chapter will guide you through various deployment strategies, focusing on ASP.NET Web API. We'll also walk you through a detailed example of deploying an ASP.NET Web API application to Azure.

Deployment Strategies

There are several ways to deploy an API:

1. **On-Premises**: Deploying on your own servers.

2. **IaaS**: Using Infrastructure-as-a-Service like AWS EC2 or Azure VMs.

3. **PaaS**: Using Platform-as-a-Service like Azure App Service or Heroku.

4. **Containers**: Using container orchestration tools like Kubernetes.

5. **Serverless**: Using serverless platforms like Azure Functions or AWS Lambda.

Each strategy has its pros and cons, and the choice often depends on your specific needs, such as scalability, control, and budget.

Pre-Deployment Checklist

Before deploying your API, make sure to:

1. **Test Thoroughly**: Ensure all endpoints are working as expected.

2. **Secure Your API**: Implement authentication and authorization.

3. **Rate Limiting**: Put in place rate limiting to prevent abuse.

4. **Logging and Monitoring**: Implement logging and set up monitoring alerts.

5. **Documentation**: Ensure your API is well-documented.

Deploying to Azure App Service

Azure App Service is a fully managed platform for building, deploying, and scaling web apps. Here's how you can deploy an ASP.NET Web API to Azure App Service.

Step 1: Create an Azure App Service

Log in to the Azure Portal and create a new App Service. Choose the operating system, runtime stack (.NET), and the region where you want your app to be hosted.

Step 2: Publish from Visual Studio

Open your ASP.NET Web API project in Visual Studio. Right-click on the project and select "Publish". Choose "Azure" as the target and select the App Service you created.

Step 3: Configuration

Before publishing, you can configure various settings like connection strings, environment variables, etc., in the "Publish" wizard.

Step 4: Deploy

Click on the "Publish" button to deploy your API. Once deployed, you'll get a URL where your API is hosted.

Adding a Custom Domain

Code Example

After deploying, you might want to add a custom domain to your API. Here's how you can do it programmatically using Azure SDK.

C#:

```csharp
using Microsoft.Azure.Management.AppService.Fluent;
using Microsoft.Azure.Management.ResourceManager.Fluent;

var credentials = SdkContext.AzureCredentialsFactory
    .FromServicePrincipal(clientId, clientSecret, tenantId, AzureEnvironment.AzureGlobalCloud);

var azure = Azure
    .Configure()
    .WithLogLevel(HttpLoggingDelegatingHandler.Level.Basic)
    .Authenticate(credentials)
    .WithDefaultSubscription();

var webApp = azure.WebApps.GetByResourceGroup(resourceGroupName, appName);

webApp.Update()
    .DefineHostnameBinding()
```

```
      .WithThirdPartyDomain(customDomainName)
      .WithSubDomain(subDomain)
      .WithDnsRecordType(CustomHostNameDnsRecordType.CName)
      .Attach()
  .Apply();
```

In this code snippet, we use Azure SDK to add a custom domain to our deployed API. Replace **clientId**, **clientSecret**, **tenantId**, **resourceGroupName**, **appName**, **customDomainName**, and **subDomain** with your specific Azure and domain details.

Conclusion

Deploying your API is a crucial step that makes it accessible to the world. Various deployment strategies can be employed depending on your specific needs. Azure App Service offers a straightforward way to deploy ASP.NET Web API applications, and with the Azure SDK, you can even automate post-deployment tasks like adding a custom domain.

Further Reading

1. "Azure for Architects" by Ritesh Modi

2. "Microservices Deployment Cookbook" by Vikram Murugesan

3. "Continuous Delivery with Docker and Jenkins" by Rafal Leszko

Chapter 13: API Documentation and Swagger

Documentation is an often overlooked but crucial aspect of API development. Good documentation not only helps developers understand how to use your API but also fosters an ecosystem around it. In this chapter, we will explore the importance of API documentation, different tools available for the task, and how to integrate Swagger with ASP.NET Web API for auto-generating documentation.

Why Documentation Matters

API documentation serves multiple purposes:

1. **Developer Onboarding**: Helps new developers understand the API quickly.

2. **Error Reduction**: Detailed documentation can significantly reduce implementation errors.

3. **Time-Saving**: Saves time during development and debugging.

4. **Community Building**: Good documentation can attract a community of developers.

Types of API Documentation

1. **Reference Documentation**: Describes every API endpoint in detail.

2. **Tutorials**: Step-by-step guides to perform specific tasks.

3. **How-To Guides**: Solutions for common problems.

4. **Conceptual Documentation**: Explains fundamental concepts and terminologies.

Tools for API Documentation

There are various tools available for API documentation, such as:

1. **Swagger**: Auto-generates documentation and provides a UI for API testing.

2. **Postman**: Allows you to create and share documentation from your Postman collections.

3. **Redoc**: Generates static HTML documentation from OpenAPI/Swagger definitions.

4. **Apiary**: Provides a platform for designing, building, and documenting APIs.

Integrating Swagger with ASP.NET Web API

Swagger is one of the most popular tools for API documentation. It can be easily integrated with ASP.NET Web API to generate real-time, interactive documentation.

Code Example

Step 1: Install NuGet Packages

First, install the following NuGet packages:

- Swashbuckle.AspNetCore

- Swashbuckle.AspNetCore.Annotations

Step 2: Configure Swagger in Startup.cs

Open **Startup.cs** and add the following code in the **ConfigureServices** method:

C#:

```csharp
using Microsoft.Azure.Management.AppService.Fluent;
using Microsoft.Azure.Management.ResourceManager.Fluent;

var credentials = SdkContext.AzureCredentialsFactory
    .FromServicePrincipal(clientId, clientSecret, tenantId, AzureEnvironment.AzureGlobalCloud);

var azure = Azure
    .Configure()
    .WithLogLevel(HttpLoggingDelegatingHandler.Level.Basic)
    .Authenticate(credentials)
    .WithDefaultSubscription();

var webApp = azure.WebApps.GetByResourceGroup(resourceGroupName, appName);
```

```
webApp.Update()
    .DefineHostnameBinding()
        .WithThirdPartyDomain(customDomainName)
        .WithSubDomain(subDomain)
        .WithDnsRecordType(CustomHostNameDnsRecordType.CName)
        .Attach()
    .Apply();
```

And in the **Configure** method:

C#:

```
app.UseSwagger();
app.UseSwaggerUI(c =>
{
    c.SwaggerEndpoint("/swagger/v1/swagger.json", "My API V1");
});
```

Step 3: Annotate Your API

You can annotate your API methods for better documentation. For example:

C#:

```
[HttpGet("{id}")]
[SwaggerOperation(Summary = "Retrieve a specific item by ID.")]
[SwaggerResponse(200, "The item was successfully retrieved.", typeof(Item))]
[SwaggerResponse(404, "The item does not exist.", typeof(void))]
public ActionResult<Item> GetItem(int id)
{
    // Your code here
}
```

Step 4: Access the Documentation

Run your application and navigate to **http://localhost:<port>/swagger** to view
the generated documentation.

Customizing Swagger UI

Code Example

You can customize the Swagger UI to better match your branding or add additional functionalities. Here's how you can add a custom CSS to the Swagger UI.

In the **Configure** method in **Startup.cs**, add:

C#:

```csharp
app.UseSwaggerUI(c =>
{
    c.SwaggerEndpoint("/swagger/v1/swagger.json", "My API V1");
    c.InjectStylesheet("/css/custom-swagger.css");
});
```

Create a **custom-swagger.css** file in the **wwwroot/css** directory and add your custom styles.

Conclusion

API documentation is an essential aspect of API development that aids in developer onboarding, reduces errors, and fosters a community. Tools like Swagger make it easy to generate interactive, real-time documentation for your ASP.NET Web API. Annotations and customizations allow you to make your documentation more informative and aligned with your branding.

Further Reading

1. "Documenting APIs: A Guide for Technical Writers" by Lucian Sova

2. "The Design of Web APIs" by Arnaud Lauret

3. "RESTful Web APIs" by Leonard Richardson, Mike Amundsen, and Sam Ruby

Chapter 14: Case Studies

Real-world examples offer invaluable insights into the practical applications of API-First Architecture using ASP.NET Web API. In this chapter, we will examine three case studies that showcase the successful implementation of API-First Architecture, discussing the challenges faced, solutions implemented, and the benefits reaped.

Case Study 1: E-commerce Platform - Shopify

Overview

Shopify is a leading e-commerce platform that allows anyone to set up an online store and sell their products. The platform has a robust API that enables third-party developers to create apps that extend the platform's functionality.

Challenges

1. **Scalability**: Handling a large number of requests from various apps.

2. **Security**: Ensuring secure transactions and data protection.

3. **Extensibility**: Allowing for easy addition of new features.

Solutions

1. **Rate Limiting**: Implemented rate limiting to control the number of API requests.

2. **OAuth2 for Authentication**: Used OAuth2 for secure authentication.

3. **Versioning**: Used API versioning to ensure backward compatibility.

Code Example

Here's an example using HttpClient to fetch a list of products from a Shopify store:

C#:

```
using System.Net.Http;
using System.Threading.Tasks;

public async Task FetchShopifyProducts()
{
    var httpClient = new HttpClient();
    httpClient.DefaultRequestHeaders.Add("X-Shopify-Access-Token", "your-access-token");

    var response = await httpClient.GetAsync("https://your-shop-name.myshopify.com/admin/api/2021-
04/products.json");
    var products = await response.Content.ReadAsStringAsync();

    // Process the products
}
```

In this example, replace "your-access-token" and "your-shop-name" with your specific details. The API call fetches the list of products in JSON format.

Case Study 2: Social Media Analytics - Hootsuite

Overview

Hootsuite is a social media management platform that offers an API for users to create custom dashboards, generate reports, and automate social media posts.

Challenges

1. **Data Consistency**: Ensuring that analytics data is consistent across all platforms.

2. **Rate Limiting**: Different social media platforms have different rate limits.

3. **Real-Time Updates**: Providing real-time analytics to users.

Solutions

1. **Data Aggregation**: Aggregated data from multiple platforms to provide unified analytics.

2. **Dynamic Rate Limiting**: Implemented dynamic rate limiting based on the platform.

3. **Webhooks for Real-Time Updates**: Used webhooks to provide real-time updates to users.

Code Example

Here's an example to schedule a message using Hootsuite's API:

C#:

```csharp
using System.Net.Http;
using Newtonsoft.Json;

public async Task ScheduleMessage()
{
    var httpClient = new HttpClient();
    httpClient.DefaultRequestHeaders.Add("Authorization", "Bearer your-access-token");

    var payload = new
    {
        text = "Hello, world!",
        socialProfileIds = new[] { "profile-id-1", "profile-id-2" },
        scheduledSendTime = "2022-01-01T12:00:00Z"
    };

    var jsonPayload = JsonConvert.SerializeObject(payload);
    var response = await httpClient.PostAsync("https://platform.hootsuite.com/v1/messages", new StringContent(jsonPayload));

    // Process the response
}
```

Replace "your-access-token", "profile-id-1", and "profile-id-2" with your specific details. This API call schedules a message to be sent at the specified time.

Case Study 3: Financial Services - Stripe

Overview

Stripe is a technology company that builds economic infrastructure for the internet. Their API allows businesses to handle payments, manage subscriptions, and perform other financial operations.

Challenges

1. **Security**: Handling sensitive financial data.

2. **Compliance**: Meeting regulatory requirements.

3. **Complexity**: Handling various payment methods and currencies.

Solutions

1. **Tokenization for Security**: Used tokenization to secure sensitive data.

2. **API for Compliance**: Provided APIs to help businesses with compliance.

3. **Multi-Currency Support**: Added support for multiple currencies via the API.

Code Example

Here's an example to create a Stripe charge using Stripe's .NET SDK:

C#:

```csharp
using Stripe;

var options = new ChargeCreateOptions
{
    Amount = 2000,
    Currency = "usd",
    Source = "tok_visa",
};

var service = new ChargeService();
Charge = service.Create(options);
```

In this example, we're creating a charge of $20. Replace "tok_visa" with an actual Stripe token.

Conclusion

These case studies demonstrate the versatility and robustness of API-First Architecture using ASP.NET Web API. They show how well-designed APIs can solve complex challenges in scalability, security, and extensibility.

Further Reading

1. "APIs: A Strategy Guide" by Daniel Jacobson, Greg Brail, and Dan Woods

2. "Building APIs You Won't Hate" by Phil Sturgeon

Chapter 15: Conclusion and Future Trends

As we reach the conclusion of this comprehensive guide on "API-First Architecture for Everything-As-A-Service development with ASP.NET Web API," it's time to reflect on the journey we've undertaken. We've explored the intricacies of API-First Architecture, delved into the technicalities of ASP.NET Web API, and examined real-world case studies. This final chapter aims to tie all these threads together and look ahead at the future trends in API development.

The Importance of API-First Architecture

The API-First Architecture has emerged as a cornerstone in modern software development. It has shifted the paradigm from monolithic applications to more modular, scalable, and flexible systems. By putting the API at the forefront of development, organizations can ensure that their software is robust, extensible, and ready to adapt to changing requirements.

Key Takeaways

Design Matters

One of the most crucial lessons is the importance of design in API development. A well-designed API not only makes it easier for developers to understand and integrate but also ensures that the API can scale and evolve without breaking existing clients.

Security is Paramount

As APIs become the gateway to critical business data and services, securing them is not just an option but a necessity. Various authentication and authorization techniques like OAuth2 and JWT can help in this regard.

Testing and Monitoring

An API is only as good as its reliability. Comprehensive testing strategies, including unit tests and integration tests, are essential for ensuring that an API performs as expected. Monitoring tools can provide real-time insights into API performance and usage patterns.

Microservices and XaaS

The rise of microservices and Everything-As-A-Service (XaaS) paradigms has further solidified the role of APIs. They act as the glue that holds these distributed systems together, enabling seamless interaction between different services and components.

Future Trends

AI and Machine Learning Integration

As Artificial Intelligence and Machine Learning continue to advance, APIs will play a crucial role in making these technologies accessible. APIs can serve as an interface for AI/ML models, allowing developers to integrate intelligent features into their applications easily.

GraphQL Over REST

While REST has been the dominant architectural style for APIs, GraphQL is gaining traction. It allows clients to request only the data they need, potentially reducing the amount of data transferred over the network.

API Gateways

The use of API Gateways is expected to rise, offering features like rate limiting, caching, and analytics. These gateways act as a single entry point for managing multiple APIs and can offer additional layers of security and efficiency.

Real-Time APIs

With the increasing demand for real-time data and notifications, WebSockets and other real-time API technologies are expected to become more prevalent.

Edge Computing

As IoT devices proliferate, the need for edge computing grows. APIs will be crucial for enabling communication between edge devices and central servers, allowing for more efficient data processing and analytics.

Final Thoughts

APIs are no longer just a technical requirement but a strategic asset that can drive business growth. An API-First approach ensures that APIs receive the attention they deserve, right from the planning phase to deployment and beyond. As technology continues to evolve, APIs will remain at the heart of digital transformation, acting as the building blocks for the next generation of software applications.

Conclusion

This book aimed to provide a holistic view of API-First Architecture and its implementation using ASP.NET Web API. We hope that the concepts, techniques, and case studies discussed have equipped you with the knowledge and confidence to embark on your API development journey. As we look forward to the future, one thing is clear: the role of APIs in software development is only going to become more significant. Thank you for joining us on this educational journey, and we wish you all the best in your future endeavors.

Further Reading

1. "The New Kingmakers" by Stephen O'Grady

2. "Continuous API Management" by Mehdi Medjaoui, Erik Wilde, Ronnie Mitra, and Mike Amundsen

Foreword

Wrapping Up

As we come to the end of this book, we hope you have gained valuable insights into the world of API-First Architecture and ASP.NET Web API. The journey may have been challenging at times, but the rewards are well worth the effort.

What Have We Accomplished?

We've covered a wide range of topics, from the basics of setting up an ASP.NET Web API project to advanced topics like security, versioning, and microservices. We've also looked at real-world case studies to understand the practical applications of the concepts discussed.

Next Steps

The world of APIs is ever-evolving, and there's always more to learn. We encourage you to continue exploring, whether it's diving deeper into ASP.NET Web API or branching out into other API technologies.

Thank You!

We want to extend our heartfelt thanks for taking the time to read this book. We hope it serves as a useful resource as you embark on your own API development journey.

This concludes our book on "API-First Architecture for Everything-As-A-Service development with ASP.NET Web API." Thank you for reading, and we hope you found it informative and useful.

www.ingramcontent.com/pod-product-compliance
Lightning Source LLC
Chambersburg PA
CBHW080939260726
48661CB00010B/3994